PICASSO

MARIO DE MICHELI

THAMES AND HUDSON

Translated from the Italian by Pearl Sanders

Published in the United States in 1989 by Thames and Hudson Inc.,
500 Fifth Avenue, New York, New York 10110

Library of Congress Catalog Card Number 89-50731

Printed in Italy

Life

Pablo Picasso was born in Malaga on 25 October 1881. His father, Jośe Ruiz Blasco, was a painter and taught drawing in the regional art school. The name Picasso was that of the artist's mother, Maria Picasso Lopez. At first, Picasso signed his works in the Spanish manner, Pablo Ruiz Picasso, but by about the year 1900 he dropped his father's surname from his signature. His first paintings reveal a most precocious talent: there is a work in Malaga Museum, *The Old Couple,* painted when Picasso was only ten years old, in 1891. While it is true that he was born into the right environment, with brushes and paints at hand from an early age, this does not in itself explain the amazing creative temperament shown in such works as *Man in a Beret, Girl with Bare Feet,* or *Interior of a Tavern,* all produced before 1898. These paintings are not merely indications of a marked 'inclination', such as any child prodigy might produce, but they are works in wich the mastery of the craft of painting is already 'professional', where the line is astonishingly sure, and the image, although still in the taste of the period, already bears the undeniable mark of the artist's individuality.

These first paintings were so impressive that Picasso's family did not show great opposition to the idea of allowing their son to follow an artistic career. He began to attend the Academy of Barcelona and then of Madrid.

Once he was in the capital, however, he preferred to visit the Prado and work on his own rather than being confined in an art school, so he interrupted his studies and began to follow his own inclination. Meanwhile in 1898 one of his paintings, *Science and Charity,* received an honourable mention at the Exhibition of Arts. The following year, on his return to Barcelona, he formed a friendship with Jaime Sabartés, who was to become his loyal secretary and affectionate biographer. Sabartés later recalled every detail of his first meeting with Picasso: the room he used as a studio in a flat where a corsetière had her workshop, the pictures on which he was working at the time, their conversation, and the moment of leavetaking: 'It is mid-day. My eyes are still full of his drawings, his albums of sketches. Picasso, who is standing, increases my confusion with the penetrating power of his bearing. On passing in front of him to take my leave, I bow slightly, affected by the magic force radiating from him. It is the marvellous power of one of the Three Wise Kings, offering gifts so rich in wonder and hope.'

At this time the circle of Picasso's friends grew wider as he came to know a group of artists and writers who frequented Les Quatre Chats (The Four Cats), a café founded by the painter Pere Romeu: this was something between a Parisian literary circle and a German beer-garden. When Picasso was not in his studio, he was at Les Quatre Chats. Various influences acted upon him at this time: El Greco and Japanese prints, the English pre-Raphaelites and the German engravers. By the beginning of 1900 Picasso's name and his drawings began to appear in the most advanced papers, *La Vanguardia, Joventud, La Catalunya Artistica*. Meanwhile he had changed his studio, and was now with his friend, the painter Carlos Casagemas, in the Calle Riera de San Juan, on the hills of the old city. He was working intensively. However, in October 1900, together with Casagemas and another friend, the painter Manuel Pallarés, he decided to go to Paris. This was his first visit to the capital of European art, and although it lasted only two months, its effects were important. It was during this short visit that Picasso met his first buyer, Berthe Weill, and sold her three paintings of the bullfight. On this same occasion he made his first contact with Pedro Manyac, the 'misguided' son of a Barcelona industrialist, who decided to pay Picasso the sum of fifty francs a month in exchange for his output.

In March 1901 in Madrid, Picasso founded a journal, *Art Joven* ('young art') for which he made numerous drawings. The journal was financed by the Catalan writer Francisco d'Asis Soler. In May, Picasso's Barcelona friends organized a one-man exhibition of his pastels in the Parés gallery. But the call of Paris was becoming more and more insistent, and Picasso set off with a load of his paintings. This time Manyac introduced him to Ambroise Vollard, whose fame as a picture dealer was spreading. Everything happened with extraordinary rapidity: on 24 June, the first Paris exhibition of Picasso's work was opened in the Rue Lafitte. There were seventy-five works, in oils and pastels: bullfights, cabaret scenes, flower paintings, variations on the theme of embracing lovers, and a series of paintings of Paris produced a few days after his arrival.

Félicien Fagus wrote an article about the exhibition in the *Gazette de l'Art,* in which he praised the talent of the young Spanish artist, while mentioning at the same time the artists who influenced him: Manet, Monet, Van Gogh, Toulouse-Lautrec, Forain... What Fagus was unable to say then, but is obvious to us today, is that some of these paintings show that Picasso was entering upon his first completely autonomous and original period, the ' blue period '.

We can consider as part of this long cycle, which extended from the end of 1901 to the end of 1904, the two works dedicated to the memory of Casagemas, who committed suicide in Paris after an unhappy love affair: *The Dead Man* and *Evocation.* During Picasso's second stay in Paris, which lasted until January 1902, he met the poet Max Jacob. From this time on, friendship with poets always had an important place in his life. Max Jacob excited Picasso's imagination and initiated him to the secrets of Montmartre and the Latin Quarter. But again he postponed settling permanently in Paris, and did not take this step until April 1904. Life was hard, but there was no turning back. During the same year, he met André Salmon, Mac Orlan and Francis Carco, and fell in love with the beautiful Fernande Olivier, who in 1933 was to write reminiscences of their bohemian existence. Daniel-Henry Kahnweiler, later Picasso's main dealer, has recalled the first time he visited Picassos's poverty-stricken studio:

' One fine day I made up my mind; I knew the address: 13 Rue Ravignan. For the first time, I mounted those stairs I was to climb so many more times... What a place Picasso had as a studio! Nobody can ever imagine the poverty, the wretchedness of those studios in the Rue Ravignan. The wallpaper was hanging in shreds from the gaping boards. The drawings were covered in dust, the canvas lay in rolls on a bottomless divan. By the stove was a sort of piled up mountain of lava: the ashes. It was appalling! This was where Picasso lived with a beautiful woman, Fernande, and a large dog called Fricka.'

In 1905 the 'pink period' began. This was the year also which saw the beginning of Picasso's friendship with the American writer Gertrude Stein and her brother Leo, the year when he formed relationships with Matisse and the poet Apollinaire, and when he became interested in Cézanne's work, then on show in a retrospective exhibition in the Salon d'Automne. Now his painting was entering on a new phase, and this reached fruition the following year in the famous masterpiece *Portrait of Gertrude Stein*. This was the dawn of Picasso's 'primitivism', also named the 'Negro period'. The outstanding work of this period is the painting to which Salmon gave the title *The Maids of Avignon*. It was begun in 1906 and completed the following year.

Around this time Picasso made the acquaintance of Rousseau, Marie Laurencin and Braque. Cubism was at hand: in the years 1908-9 the paintings produced by Picasso at Creil and Horta de Ebro in Spain, together with those done by Braque at l'Estaque, initiated the period of 'heroic' cubism, which was followed until 1912 by what has been called 'analytical' cubism, and then, until about 1920, by 'synthetic' cubism.

But many other things occurred in those years. There were new meetings: with Juan Gris and Marcoussis (1910); with Jacques Villon, Marcel Duchamps, Gleizes, Metzinger, Delaunay and Léger (1912); with Cocteau (1916). New loves: Marcelle Hubert (1912) and Olga Khoklova, whom he met in Rome in 1916 when he went to see Diaghilev's ballets for which he had designed the scenery. New artistic events: his first American exhibition, in New York (1910); the beginning of *papiers collés* (1912); the publication of Apollinaire's book *Les peintres cubistes* (1913); the one-man show of cubist works in the Paul Rosenberg Gallery (1919). In 1913, the year before the outbreak of war, Picasso's father died in Barcelona; the war took from him his great friend Apollinaire, who died in Paris in 1919 as the result of a war wound. The post-war period saw the development of Picasso's neoclassical painting. He began to paint in this way in 1915 and continued to do so at the same time as he produced his cubist works. One of the most frequently recurring themes of the neoclassical paintings is motherhood. It was a subject he had constantly before him at that time, as Olga was then expecting the birth of Picasso's first child, who was born in February 1921 and named Paul. Picasso moved about so much during those years that it would take too long to record all his movements here. Mention must be made, however, of his stay at Juan-les-Pins, on the Mediterranean, in the spring and summer of 1920; this was the beginning of a new creative season in his art, the season of myths, which has endured until the present day. From then on the sea called to him unceasingly, and in 1922 he settled there.

Until 1924 he continued to work on theatre designs: the last was for the ballet *Mercury* commissioned by Count Etienne de Beaumont to music by Satie and choreography by Massine. In the same year another important meeting took place: with André Breton, who had just published his *Surrealist Manifesto*. They met at Cap d'Antibes, and through Breton Picasso came to know the other young members of the surrealist group.

In 1928 he returned to sculpture and produced a number of wire constructions. ' Returned ' is the right word, because his interest in sculpture was not new; over the years he had created many pieces which are certainly the equals of his best paintings. We need think only of *The Jester,* of 1905 (*ill. on p. 9*), *The Glass of Absinthe* of 1914, the metal *Construction* of 1930, the *Bull's Head* and *Cock* of 1932 (*ill. on p. 27*), the *Cat* of 1941, the *Man with Lamb* of 1944 (*ill. on p. 29*), the *Goat* of 1950 (*ill. on p. 31*). But at the time of which we are speaking, and especially after 1930, Picasso began to take a great interest in engraving year in the famous masterpiece *Portrait of Gertrude Metamorphoses;* for Vollard, he illustrated Balzac's *Chef-d'Oeuvre Inconnu* in 1931; and in 1933-4 he engraved forty-five plates illustrating classical subjects, which were published under the title *The Sculptor's Studio*, as well as the *Minotaur* series.

The year 1934 was decisive for Picasso's art: it was the year of his return to Spain with Maria Teresa Walter, a beautiful woman whom he had met casually in the street three years earlier. They travelled to Irun, San Sebastian, Madrid and Toledo. It was a long and thrilling journey, during which Picasso discovered as if for the first time the energy, violence and vitality of his native land. It was this impassioned contact with Spain in that year which made him so fervent a supporter of the cause of the Spanish Republic. In the early days of the Spanish Civil War, which broke out in July 1936, the government appointed Picasso director of the Prado museum. On 8 and 9 January of the following year, he wrote his invective against Franco: *Sueño y Mentira de Franco* ('dream and lie of Franco'). 'Fandango of screech-owls, salamoya of swords, of octopus, of ill-augur, tearing of tonsured hair...' This was published with some engravings of Picasso's.

He had begun to write assiduously in 1935, at a time when his disagreements with his wife Olga began to affect his paintings very badly. These disagreements led soon afterwards to the complete break-up of their marriage. In the same year, a girl, Maia, was born to Maria Teresa Walter. However, another encounter was soon to take place: with Dora Maar, whose portrait he painted countless times.

Picasso was in Paris when he heard the news of the bombing of Guernica by the Fascists on 28 April 1937. His dismay and anger were expressed in a series of drawings and paintings which became the nucleus of the vast tempera to be named after the martyred Basque town. Two months later, in June, the masterpiece was completed. In his studio in the Rue des Grands-Augustins, Dora Maar made photographic records of the various stages in the production of this vast composition. In the same month it was exhibited in the Spanish Pavilion of the Paris International Exhibition.

In 1939 the Museum of Modern Art in New York organized a great Picasso exhibition, which established his fame on the other side of the Atlantic. But while he was enjoying this triumph, there came the news of his mother's death in Barcelona and, in September, the outbreak of the second World War. In the summer, which he spent at Antibes, Picasso produced a light-hearted painting: *Night Fishing at Antibes*. With the War and the invasion of France, his paintings assumed more and more a tragic character. Picasso returned to Paris in 1940 and remained there

The Jester (see note on p. 33)

throughout the War. In 1941 he wrote a lyrical-grotesque comedy entitled *Le Désir attrapé par la queue* ('Desire Caught by the Tail'), which was read in the house of the Leiris couple by an exceptional group of performers including Camus, Sartre, Simone de Beauvoir and Reymond Queneau. During this period he turned again to sculpture, and in February 1942, after many preparatory studies, he produced one of his best-known masterpieces, *The Man with a Lamb*, now in the main square at Vallauris. It was at that time that he met Françoise Gilot, who gave him two children: Claude, born in May 1947, and Paloma, born in April 1949. But there was more bad news to come too: in February 1944 Max Jacob died in a German prison, and many other friends died in that terrible time. It was the anguish of those years that led Picasso to paint a work expressing his horror of war: *The Charnel House*.

But the end of the war came at last and the liberation was joyously celebrated in the streets and squares of Paris. Picasso joined the French Communist Party, and explained his reasons in an article which he sent to the American journal *New Masses*: 'I was so eager to find a homeland again: I have always been an exile, now I am one no longer.' After the liberation, Picasso's painting became more serene. He was devoured by a new urge to work and produce. He also wished to experiment with new techniques.. The year before, he had enthusiastically taken up lithography; now, in 1947, in the Madoura factory in Vallauris, pottery claimed his enthusiasm, and in the course of ten or twelve months no fewer than two thousand pieces came from his prodigious hands.

His first exhibition of pottery – 150 works – was held in the Maison de la Pensée in Paris in 1948. In August of that year, together with Eluard and Vercors, he participated in the Congress of Intellectuals for Peace, held at Wroclaw in Poland. The following year he went to Rome for the same purpose. This was the year also when he produced for Aragon the lithograph of the famous *Dove*, to be published with the manifesto of the World Peace Congress. In summer 1950 he painted in the same spirit *Massacre in Korea*, and in 1952, the *War* and *Peace* paintings at Vallauris.

The year 1953 saw his separation from Françoise Gilot and the death of Eluard. In the following year Matisse also died, and in 1955 Picasso's wife Olga Khoklova died in Cannes. Picasso was approaching his seventy-fifth birthday. His energy amazed everyone who came into contact with him. In December 1954 he worked on the theme of Delacroix' *Women of Algiers*, and produced fifteen variations on the famous painting. In the earlier part of the same year, he made some hundreds of drawings on the subject of the artist and model, a subject to wich he returned in 1963.

Meanwhile, still in 1954, a new love affair began. The year before, he had met Jacqueline Roque, the cousin of Madame Ramié who owned the pottery factory where he worked, and he married her in February 1958. He left Vallauris in 1955 and moved to the hills of Cannes, to the Villa Californie; in 1959 he moved again, this time to a castle in the Cose valley near Aix-en-Provence; in 1961 he went to Mas Notre-Dame-de-Vie at Mougins.

Through all these upheavals, Picasso's work did not suffer any interruption; in 1957 he produced about twenty versions of *Las Meninas* of Velázquez, then in February 1958, the large mural for the new U N E S C O building in Paris, and in 1961, the many drawings and paintings inspired by Manet's *Luncheon on the Grass*.

In the years since the war, there have been several large retrospective exhibitions of Picasso's work, the most important of which by far are the Rome and Milan exhibitions held in 1953, the London exhibition of 1960, the exhibitions held in Canada and Japan in 1964, and finally, the vast retrospective exhibition in Paris at the Grand Palais and the Petit Palais in November 1966, where it was possible to retrace Picasso's entire artistic itinerary through a choice of 280 paintings, 200 drawings, 180 sculptures and 115 ceramics. The exhibition was officially organized by the French Government and the city of Paris in homage to Picasso on his eighty-fifth birthday.

No celebrations were allowed to interrupt his work. Even at ninety his energy was unabated. As he once said to Sabartés, 'Work is a therapy.' For Picasso this remained true until, on 8 April 1973, the end came at last.

Works

Among Picasso's countless spoken utterances, recorded by benevolent or malevolent biographers, there is one from the period after the Second World War, which throws an especially vivid light on his attitude to painting and his method of confronting problems.

' I paint as others write their autobiographies. My paintings, whether they are finished or not, are the pages of my diary and are valid as such. The future will choose the pages it prefers. It is not up to me to do so. I feel as though time is slipping away from me more and more quickly. I am like a river which continues to flow, carrying with it the trees growing too close to the banks, abandoned carcases, and the various species of microbes proliferating in its waters. I drag all this along with me and go on my way. It is the movement of painting which interests me, the dramatic passage from one endeavour to another, even though these endeavours may not be carried through to their conclusion. In the case of some of my works, I can say without any doubt that the endeavour has been carried to its conclusion, since I have succeeded in blocking the flow of life around me. I have less and less time, yet I have always more to say. And what I have to say is, more and more, something which moves forward together with the movement of my thought. '

These words contain all Picasso's awareness of himself as a creative force, subject to every contradiction of life and history; they also reveal his belief that he possesses a natural energy which can have no rest, but is destined to advance with an irresistible force, through every difficulty. But there is also the anxiety arising from the urgency of the need for expression, from the choice of the images in which the meaning of our existence is to be illuminated in new and unexpected ways. This must never be forgotten when we think of Picasso. Through the filter of his most singular personality, Picasso has succeeded, as perhaps no other artist ever has, in placing on fiery record the themes of anguish and fury, ferocity and heroism, idyll and desperation, which lie at the root of present-day life. Picasso's personal destiny is deeply interwoven with this historical and at the same time existential predicament. This is why his paintings and images are always concerned with ideas and passions which go far beyond the terms of a pure aestheticism. And this is also why, on more than one occasion, he has appeared in the centre of violent polemics, where not only the values of art were under discussion, but the values of man, in his choices and his acts.

Picasso is not a 'moderate' but a 'radical' of painting, a root-and-branch revolutionary. A painting such as *The Maids of Avignon* (*pl. 13*), which he produced at the age of twenty-five, between the end of 1906 and the spring of 1907, is a 'radical' work. What is left here of the traditional view of painting? Perspective is broken, shattered completely; colour has lost all atmosphere and become arid and lifeless; the figures are made up of angles fitted together. The revolt against the clichés of painting is complete.

'What I would like to make people feel,' writes Kahnweiler, 'is the incredible heroism of a man like Picasso. There was a cruel element in his moral solitude at that time, because none of his painter friends followed him. The picture he had produced seemed to everyone an insane and monstrous thing. Braque, who had become acquainted with Picasso through Apollinaire, said the impression it made on him was as if someone had drunk petroleum so as to spit fire, while Derain said to me privately that we would soon find Picasso hanging behind his large painting, so desperate did its mood seem to him.'

Yet, at least until the first half of 1905, it seemed unbelievable that Picasso's painting would reach such a stage only a year later. The so-called 'blue period', with which he had broken away from previous influences in 1902, contained no hint of such an outcome. This period of Picasso's painting had been imbued with pathos and warm humanity, and populated with beggars, grieving mothers and sick children, figures bathed in a gentle bluish tonality; it was a world of heartbreaking sadness. Then, as the blue tones became lighter, and a new hint of colour began to appear,

13

circus people became the favourite subjects of his paintings: young acrobats, slender dancers, agile bareback riders, clowns and harlequins dressed in patchwork costumes. This was the beginning of the 'pink period', in 1905. The desolate tone of the previous works yielded to a more resigned mood of gentle melancholy.

Picasso's position at this time was curious: this was the very year when the colour of the fauves burst upon the world, yet his palette continued to be exceptionally restrained, even when it grew lighter and incorporated some new colour elements. Even when painting a harlequin costume, Picasso preferred cold and almost colourless tones. As for the circus and its acrobats, this was a literary theme which was appreciated by his poet friends Max Jacob and Guillaume Apollinaire. Cézanne himself had painted harlequins. The culmination of the pink period, the painting which most effectively sums up its achievement is without doubt *Circus People* (*Saltimbanques*) now in the National Gallery, Washington. Not even in this work is there the slightest indication of what was to come soon after, in *The Maids of Avignon*. Yet from the middle of the year 1905 something was changing in Picasso's inspiration and attitude to his subjects. If, in fact, we observe his treatment of a theme such as that of young boys leading horses to water, or girls combing their hair, which together came to replace the circus themes, we see that from this time until the beginning of 1906 stylistic and other innovations gradually made their appearance. Now the diffused tonality gave way to a concentration of colour within the forms, while the drawing became more boldly outlined, so as to make the figures stand out from the background in sharper relief; the horses were painted in a layer of ash colour, the young naked bodies modelled in reddish-brown, while the earth was scorched like a dune. Every element was modelled and constructed with the greatest concentration on essential features. *Boy with a Horse* (Museum of Modern Art, New York) is certainly one of the most explicit examples of this transformation in Picasso's style.

But this was not all: the transformation was not one of style alone. Changes in style are in effect indications of a movement towards a new vision. In these horses being led to the river by their young riders, freed from the shackles of civilization, there can be found the aspiration to purity and innocence which since 1870 had been associated with Rimbaud and Gauguin. The echo of Rimbaud's cry ' Become savages ' can be heard behind these new images of Picasso. And it was not only in Picasso that this echo was resounding, but among a large group of other artists as well. This cry sums up the artists' rejection of both ' constituted society' and official art; in short, it represents a revolt against a situation which was now far removed from the ideas and sentiments that had nourished the greatest minds only fifty years before. The discovery of the ' primitive ' is the direct consequence of this revolt, and without this discovery Picasso would not have painted *The Maids of Avignon*.

But before he came to this painting, Picasso again passed through a series of stylistic phases which can be recapitulated by mentioning three works produced in 1906: *Portrait of Gertrude Stein* (*pl. 12*); *Self-portrait*; *Two Nudes*. We need only compare the structure of these images to realize how far now were the vaguely humanitarian and elegiac cadences which had dominated the blue and pink period works. Here we are in a harsh, unbending and barbaric world. The influences of archaic and Negro sculpture upon his style are obvious, although Picasso has attempted to deny that this is the case. However, for Picasso the discovery of the ' primitive ' goes far beyond the simple acquisition of certain stylistic innovations or a mere delight in exoticism. In contrast to many artists for whom the primitive has been more an opportunity for cultural or social polemic, or a purely aesthetic exercise, for Picasso it was something which enabled him to discover his real nature and to express himself without the impediment of conventions or inhibitions. In his view, primitivism means above all spontaneity, reliance on impulses and passions, going beyond any rule or formula.

The Maids of Avignon (*pl. 13*) is the result of all this. This painting was the first great example of that ' fury ', at once cerebral and instinctive, which is so typical of Picasso's

15

nature. In this canvas there is a primordial force, which was to endure for at least two years and be expressed in a series of angular still-lifes, as well as in a group of imposing volumetric figures and landscapes. At Horta de Ebro in 1909 this early violence abated, Cézanne's teaching was heeded, and the geometric forms became calmer and less distorted. This was the real beginning of cubism.

Volume and structure were Picasso's two prime considerations in his cubist paintings, as they were for Braque also. By eliminating atmosphere, sensuous colour and curving lines, they aimed at producing painting of elemental vigour. This was their reaction against impressionism and, later, against fauvism with its excessive emphasis on colour. In the early stages of cubism, colour took second place and neutral tones predominated: greys, earth colours, pale greens. At the end of the year 1909 there began what has been named 'analytical cubism': the 'heroic' cubism of the first phase, which was literally built up of 'cubes', simple, broad, volumetric planes, which still somehow produced images of reality arranged in depth, was followed by a form of cubism in which the planes were further broken up into a continous dense mass of small planes which took the object completely apart – 'analysed' it – and arranged it on the surface of the canvas, where relief was now reduced to a minimum. The special features of this stage of cubism can be appreciated in such works as *Portrait of Daniel-Henry Kahnweiler*, 1910, *Mandoline Player*, 1911 (*pl. 18*), and *Spanish Still-life*, 1912 (*pl. 19*).

In a later stage of development, towards the end of 1912, 'analytical cubism' gave way to 'synthetic cubism'. A fundamental element of 'synthetic' cubism was the free reconstruction of the object once it was finally released from perspective; the object was no longer analysed and taken apart, but was presented in its essential being, without any suggestion of photographic representation. The synthesis was applied to the whole of the object or only to certain parts, and several profiles were shown on the canvas. This freedom marked the end also of the straight line and lifeless colours. The line became more flexible and the colours, while remaining pure and non-atmospheric, began to glow. *Woman in a*

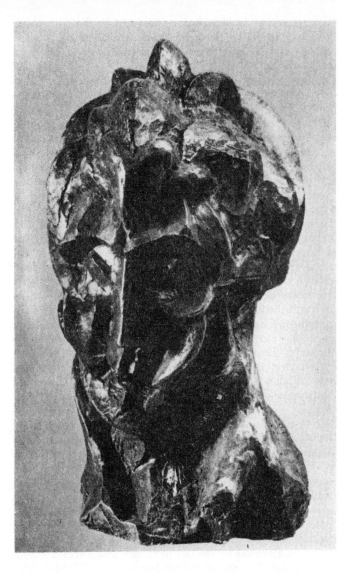

Head of Woman (see note on p. 33)

Chemise seated in an Armchair, painted in the autumn of 1913, represents an important stage in this new period of cubism, into which a new element was soon to be introduced: collage.

This new technique, which has been so important in contemporary art, appeared as early as 1912. It has been interpreted in very many different ways. Apollinaire gave a somewhat sentimental interpretation: in his view, the application of postage stamps, waxed cloth, wallpaper, envelopes and other material to canvas or paper, among other painted colours, was to introduce an element already 'long imbued with humanity' enriching the work with a new pathos and creating a contrast between truth and artifice. In fact, it would be more correct to say that collage was for the cubists one way of reacting against the picturesque, and of finding a new way of interpreting nature without the use of brush strokes. Whatever its purpose, collage was a new means of expression, and Picasso showed consummate mastery of the technique, without bothering overmuch with the theory behind it.

This anti-theoretical attitude of Picasso should be stressed, as it throws light on the particular position he held within the cubist movement. He once said: 'Mathematics, trigonometry, chemistry, psychoanalysis, music, and goodness knows what else, have all been brought in to explain cubism. All this has been nothing but words, non-sense, and has produced the evil result that it has blinded people with science.'

Picasso could not accept the kind of neo-Platonic or vaguely phenomenological interpretation of cubism which Gleizes and Metzinger gave, and which was to lead later to the abstract neo-Plasticism of Mondrian. Cubism represented for Picasso, among other things, the kind of formal discipline and rigour he needed to contain the tumultuous emotion behind *The Maids of Avignon* within an intellectually ordered pattern. However, the narrow formulas of cubism could not satisfy him completely. He had already begun to extend its frontiers by the use of colour which was anything but cerebral, but this was still not enough. The fact was that his pink period had been exhausted too quickly, and he still felt the stimulus of the kind of image which had inspired him then. The revolt against tradition had not completely killed his aspiration towards natural beauty, represented so movingly by young boys with horses and by girls before a mirror. So it happened that at the height of the cubist period, like a hidden spring rising unexpectedly to the surface, there returned to his memory the youthful bodies of the riders and the untamed grace of the young girls he had painted ten or eleven years before.

The first signs of this recollection appear in a group of drawings of 1914-15. These drawings mark the beginning of his 'neoclassical' period, when in a series of portraits he returned to the line of Ingres, that penetrating, exact and unwavering line which is the great fascination of his art. The choice of Ingres as a comparison is not fortuitous: there are people who consider, and not without reason, that cubism itself is a classical form of art. That is why both Ingres and David have always appealed to the cubists. In Picasso, however, this was something more than a matter of taste: it was a force which impelled him towards a harmony, no sooner perceived than shattered again in a thousand ways, without for that reason being any less deeply felt.

It is difficult to state with any certainty where this influence arose, especially because in the case of Picasso every hint or suggestion from other sources was re-created with the spontaneity of original creation. However, there can be no doubt that his visit to Italy in 1916 left him with a feeling for massiveness of scale, the imaginative grandeur of a Michelangelo. Perhaps in Italy he came to understand that his impetus and creative force could now attempt the 'grand manner' and find in it a hitherto unkown release. This had its effect not only on his neoclassical painting, but on other forms as well, and gave him a new sense of freedom in which his imagination could expand. The early neoclassical painting then changed considerably, as the line of Ingres lost some of its analytical penetration and acquired instead spatial quality. No longer was Picasso attracted by the slender, graceful bodies of adolescents, but by sumptuous women, matronly and monumental. This was in the year

1920, the year when Picasso went to stay on the Mediterranean coast of France, in the region which was from then on to become his 'ideal'. It was here that he began to produce drawings and paintings of women abandoned to the happy idleness of a mythical existence: women reclining softly on the sand, or running wildly along the shore, intent on the care of their beauty, or emerging out of the water. The nude figures are heavy and large, some of them enormous, others less massive, but always drawn extremely freely, often with daring distortions or even total deformations of anatomical exactitude, so that they could not be understood if the ideas of cubism were not known. The feeling of primordial nature returns in these nudes, they tend to assume the character of sublime symbols of life, almost as if they were nature goddesses. It was in a similar spirit that at this time also Picasso treated the subject of the mother and child in many paintings.

It should not be forgotten, however, that the years of neoclassicism, especially from 1920 to 1924, were also the years of what has been called the 'great cubist period', the period of the masked musicians and of the still-lifes with musical instruments. Some of these works are among the finest Picasso ever painted. They no longer have the tight structure of preceding cubist works but are conceived with greater breadth and simplicity, and less schematically. The influence of neoclassicism can clearly be seen in these works, just as, on the other hand, the knowledge gained through cubism enabled Picasso to achieve great sculptural effects within the classical forms. There is a still-life painted in 1919, *Chest of Drawers* (*pl. 26*), which might be considered a middle term between the two experiences: the heavily folded tablecloth, the square and stumpy shape of the bread, the volumetric roundness of the fruit, the robust solidity of the flower stems, the free decorative rhythm of the stucco work on the background wall, draw from both the expansive forms of neoclassicism and the synthesis of cubism. In other works, such as the two large versions of *Three Musicians* (*pl. 29*), the points of contact are less obvious: in these the colours are flat and brilliant, whereas in the monumental works it is more subdued and subtle; the composition too is based on geometric forms; yet some connection remains.

The great cubist period, together with the neoclassical period, constitute two of the most fruitful aspects of Picasso's art. This is true especially because as they acted upon each other in turn, they later became the basis for all his future work and opened the way to a complete freedom of expression from which ' periods ' were to disappear and in which every previous fact, discovery and indication was automatically absorbed into a superior and autonomous process of creation.

It was at this stage, about 1925, that Picasso first came into contact with the surrealists. He has always denied being a surrealist painter, and when we consider surrealist works in general it is difficult not to agree with him. Yet there can be no doubt that his contacts with surrealism stimulated him and led to greater freedom of expression and a more immediate manner of revealing through line and colour the depths of the unconscious. It is true, of course, that Picasso rejected the automatic element in surrealism and its random invention of images, but he did not fail to grasp its most essential feature: the poetic intuition of the unconscious, the revelation of a world, buried within ourselves, which nevertheless plays such a crucial part in determining our actions.

This was a difficult time in Picasso's private life. He and his wife Olga found it more and more difficult to get on together. Perhaps this was partly, or mainly, what induced him at this time to explore his mind and his psychological difficulties, at the root of which he found the anarchic instincts of sex linked with impulses of cruelty and sadism. This is the subterranean region which, between 1925 and 1933, and even later, Picasso succeeded in revealing with an extraordinary outspokenness. Now the neoclassical and cubist forms were submitted to a thorough-going expressionist treatment, which contorted and deformed them, built them up only to tear them apart again, thus originating a form of painting which corresponds very closely to the epithet ' convulsive ', identified by Breton with the term ' beauty '.

The female figure became reduced to disturbing forms of aggressive libido, tormented and tortured forms, in which desire and vengeance, greed and repulsion, pain and revolt, appear in a turmoil hitherto unknown in Picasso's art. The neoclassical theme of women on the sea shore still attracted him, but now the women were identified with symbols of sexual obsession.

When Picasso returned to Spain in 1934, his personal difficulties had in part been overcome. His renewed contact with Spain had an extraordinarily powerful effect upon him and he felt again all the ardour and violence of his native land. His early enthusiasms returned: bullfights, cock-fight-ding and popular spectacles. He loved everything exciting, heroic or tragic that he found in those surroundings. There

Head
(see note on p. 35)

was nothing picturesque about Picasso's Spain. Now at last the urgent power which had guided his hand while he painted *The Maids of Avignon* flowed back into his blood and was liberated in new drawings and canvases, enriched with all his later experiences. Now he painted fighting cocks, horses wounded in the bull ring, bulls run through by the sword, and the theme of the Minotaur, which he had begun to paint a year previously, acquired a complex significance of brutality and tenderness, violence and pity.

It was this wealth of images and feelings that lay at the origin of *Guernica* (*pl. 43*). From the point of view of the constituent elements of its composition, this great tempera, painted in the days following the terrible bombing raid in 1937, was all to be found already in the *Minotauromachy* engravings done two years earlier: the bull, the horse, the light, the house, the window, the wounded woman. But in many drawings and paintings of 1934-5 it is possible to trace even more closely not only a coincidence of details in the subject matter, but also analogous or completely identical forms of expression, as in the drawing dated 15 April 1935, or certain canvases of the same period, where Picasso represented the instant of the bull striking against the horse, but especially in the engravings for *Sueño y Mentira de Franco*.

Of course, the material which he had already used in these other works was treated quite differently in *Guernica*, in terms of anger and tragedy. Here we are at the summit of Picasso's creative tension. The statement of his vision did not even need colour: the definite and precise terms of black and white sufficed to express all that was needed. The painting has its own pitiless logic: its outlines are as sharp as a sword, the shade and light split the spaces asunder, the characters perform gestures of contained energy. At a time when European painting was tending more and more to a pure subjectivism or decorativeness, Picasso reinvented in *Guernica* the 'historical painting' and demonstrated the possibility of an art directly concerned with human affairs. Numerous preparatory studies and autonomous works are related to *Guernica*. Among these is the series of *Weeping Women* (*pl. 44*). The same use of black and white and of cutting outlines found in *Guernica* was adopted again by Picasso in another very important work, dated 1944-5 and unfinished: *The Charnel House,* a work inspired by the horror of the concentration camps.

The series of *Seated Women* (*pl. 49*), painted throughout the Second World War, continued to express Picasso's tragic mood, but the forms were more sculptural and varied and the images more indirect. The apprehensions and fears, the fury and rancour, which were part of Picasso's psychological condition during the whole period of the German occupation of France, found their outlet in these paintings. In a sense they recall the surrealist 'monsters', but they were really very different: at the time of surrealism the monsters arose from the depths of the artist's being, whereas now they corresponded to an objective reality; they were in fact 'historical monsters'. In other words, the contempt for the human appearance which was apparent in these works was symbolic of the denial of humanity which the forces of evil were perpetrating in the countries of Europe. Speaking of these paintings, Picasso later said: 'I did not paint the war, because I am not one of those painters who go around like photographers looking for a subject, but there is no doubt that in the pictures I painted at that time the war is present'.

A work which is the 'reverse' of *Guernica* and of all the other tragic paintings, is *Joie de Vivre,* completed in 1946. The hard days of war were over and Picasso felt the rebirth of a new excitement. He again experienced a desire for life, love and freedom in nature. Back in the South of France, the Mediterranean myths recaptured his imagination; this time, however, his inspiration was more lyrical.

In *Joie de Vivre* the dancing nymph is outlined in melodic and sensual curves, while the flute-playing faun and centaur are drawn in a more concise but equally agile and sure line. Only the sea, sky and earth are the background for these figures – a dazed and stupefied nature, arrested under the spell of the music, one instant before the beginning of spring's awakening. The blue, yellow and lilac colours merge and bathe the scene in a festive glow which seems to diffuse a naturalistic pleasure in light.

Picasso painted this work in a happy mood, his mind free of all anguish. No element arrests the flow of its joyous rhythm. It is a picture which seems to have painted itself, so spontaneous is it, and so absent from its expression is any sign of creative effort. Few works can have communicated, as this does, the almost physical sense of joy in a Pan-like embrace of nature. The only great precedent of this order of inspiration is Picasso's *Night Fishing at Antibes,* painted a month before the outbreak of war; but where that painting contained only a calm contentment, here there is dithyrambic joy.

Joie de Vivre, like *Guernica,* and in fact any of Picasso's important works, stands at the centre of a great number of paintings and drawings which continue or repeat the same themes. All these works stress particularly the aspect of idyll, of aspiration towards integrity, of vital liberation of the emotions, which form one of the basic components of Picasso's art, just as *Guernica* and the works connected with it show most clearly the sombre side of Picasso's genius, the dramatic and tragic aspect.

Both these facets of his inspiration were treated at the same time in two vast murals: *War (pls 61-3)* and *Peace (pl. 60).* These are two modern allegories, in which Picasso has used the gifts of his fantasy in a new way. In *War,* which is a horizontal composition, the faun of *Joie de Vivre* has become a fateful god of destruction with bat's wings decorated with skulls. From the top of a funerary chariot he scatters around him the germs of bacteriological warfare, while the horses pulling the chariot, painted in brush strokes of putrescent green, are stamping on an open book, as symbols of anti-culture; the procession of the shades of ancient warriors along the background reminds us that war is at the very roots of humanity's history. At the left edge of the composition, the solemn figure of the defender of peace rises up, bearing a shield with the design of a dove. The *Peace* panel is more varied in its composition, and references to *Joie de Vivre,* as well as other sources, are even more explicit.

While he was working on these two great panels, Picasso said to Kahnweiler: 'I must make the Temple of Peace while I am still capable of clambering up the stairs'. At the time he was just over seventy years of age. Fifteen and more years have passed since then, and there are no signs of the weight of age in Picasso's work. He has continued to create new images with inexhaustible vigour. We need think only of his 'variations' on Delacroix' *Women of Algiers* (1954-5), on *Las Meninas* of Velazquez (1958-9), or on Manet's *Déjeuner sur l'Herbe,* 1960 (*pls 70-72*), or the series of canvases painted in 1962 on the theme of the *Rape of the Sabines* (*pl. 73*) and the large number of *Artist and Model* paintings of 1963 (*pls 77-9*). We were given abundant evidence of Picasso's lifetime of tireless energy in the rooms of the Grand and Petit Palais in Paris on the occasion of the vast retrospective exhibition held in November 1966 in celebration of his eighty-fifth birthday. The most recent works, painted in mid-1965 (female nudes, heads of men, landscapes) reveal a fresh and youthful spirit which amazes everyone. Not only does Picasso not seem ' tired ', he seems to be on the threshold of something new: the creation of works of art in which painting is pursued to its inmost essence in an ultimate lyrical synthesis. The work of seventy years, and the knowledge and experience gained during those years, have left their mark on these most recent works, in which Picasso finds a totally spontaneous language. When we look at these works, we realize that the whole of his previous experience, all the periods and styles through which he has' passed, have merged into an individual art which knows nothing of schools or formulae. And it may be that these latest works help us to understand the earlier Picasso as well. They reveal the constant element in Picasso's art, that poetic and expressive truth which is alive within his eclecticism, the multiplicity and contemporaneity of his styles, imprinting each moment of his activity with its own unmistakable individuality. Picasso once said to a friend that he is a painter ' without a style '. It is easier for us now to understand what he meant. This is that he is a painter so open to the impact of reality, in all its violence, that he obeys the emotions which reality arouses in him at different times, refusing to imprison them within the preconceived scheme of any style.

This continual readiness to receive emotion from the world and from mankind is the secret of Picasso's vitality and the reason behind every one of his changes. This is what constitutes his personal language. 'Without order, without disorder, with simplicity', wrote Eluard in an attempt to define the special quality of this language. But Picasso himself, in a famous declaration. said that the painter must be 'constantly awake to the lacerating, the ardent and the pleasant happenings of the world' and demonstrated the necessity for the artist to 'model himself totally in their image'. That is why there is no metaphysical nostalgia in Picasso.

Gertrude Stein, during the cubist years, stated that he was too taken up with 'things' to be concerned with the 'spirit'. Mauriac has even spoken of his 'superhuman hatred of the soul'. Everything in his work is subordinated to the prime importance of objective reality, a reality which wounds and lacerates him, but which at the same time penetrates into his inmost being. There, without a doubt, lies the secret of Picasso's greatness, and of his unflagging creative force.

Cock (see note on p. 35)

27

Picasso and the Critics

A forest of essays, books, articles, poems, memoirs and film documentaries has grown up around Picasso and his work. He is without any doubt the present-day artist about whom most has been written, and who has given rise to the greatest amount of discussion and polemics. Not all of this criticism is serious; often it is frivolous or superficial, treating him as no more than a ' man in the news '. But there are many serious works as well, which make an important contribution to a knowledge of Picasso and his art. The following short list will be found useful. It is arranged in order of contents, beginning with Picasso's own writings and continuing with books of reminiscences, biographies, monographs, catalogues and essays.

BY PICASSO

Scritti di Picasso, edited by M. De Micheli, Milan 1964.

REMINISCENCES

Max Jacob, *Souvenirs sur Picasso*, Cahiers d'Art, Paris 1927; Fernande Olivier, *Picasso et ses amis*, Stock, Paris 1933; Gertrude Stein, *Autobiography of Alice B. Toklas*, Harcourt Brace, New York 1933; Jaime Sabartés, *Portraits et souvenirs*, Louis Carré and Maximilien Vox, Paris 1946; H. Parmelin, *Picasso sur place*, Julliard, Paris 1959; André Salmon, *Souvenirs sans fin,* Gallimard, Paris 1955; Ilya Ehrenburg, *Lyudi, gody, zhizn'* (' People, years, life '), Moscow 1960; D. H. Kahnweiler, *Confessions esthétiques*, Gallimard, Paris 1963; H. Parmelin, *Les Dames de Mougins,* Cercle d'Art, Paris 1964; *Le peintre et son Modèle,* Cercle d'Art, Paris 1966; *Notre Dame de Vie,* Cercle d'art, Paris 1966; Françoise Gilot and Carleton Lake, *Life with Picasso,* McGraw-Hill, London 1964; Brassaï, *Picasso & Co.,* Thames and Hudson, London 1967.

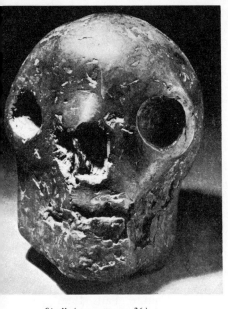

Skull (see note p. 36)   *Man with Lamb (see note p. 36)*

BIOGRAPHIES

A. Vallentin, *Picasso*, Editions Albin Michel, Paris 1957;
Roland Penrose, *Picasso - His life and work*, Victor Gollancz, London 1958.

MONOGRAPHS AND SPECIAL STUDIES

Maurice Raynal, *Picasso*, Crés, Paris 1922; Jean Cocteau,
Picasso, Stock, Paris 1923, re-issued in *Le rappel à l'ordre,*
Stock, Paris 1926; Pierre Reverdy, *Pablo Picasso*, NRF,
Paris 1924; Wilhelm Uhde, *Picasso et la tradition française*,
Paris 1928; R. G. de la Serna, *Ismos*, Biblioteca Nueva,
Madrid 1931; Eugenio d'Ors, *Pablo Picasso*, Paris 1930;
Christian Zervos, *Pablo Picasso*, Hoepli, Milan 1932; Gertrude Stein, *Picasso*, Librairie Floury, Paris 1938; J. Merli,
Picasso, el artista y la obra de nuestro tiempo, Buenos Aires 1942; A. Cirici-Pellicer, *Picasso antes de Picasso*, Iberia-

Jaquin Gil, Barcelona 1946; Alfred H. Barr, Jr., *Picasso - Fifty Years of His Art,* Museum of Modern Art, New York 1946; W. Boeck (with preface by Sabartés), *Picasso,* Flammarion, Stuttgart 1955; D. D. Duncan, *Picasso's Picassos,* Lausanne 1961; R. Arnhein, *Picasso's Guernica, The Genesis of a Painting,* University of California 1962; Pierre Daix and Georges Boudaille, *Picasso 1900-1906,* Neuchâtel and Paris 1966.

Catalogues

Christian Zervos, *Oeuvres,* Cahiers d'Art, Paris 1932-66: this is the complete catalogue of Picasso's works between 1895 and 1957, with 8,220 illustrations of pictures and drawings. F. Russoli, *Pablo Picasso,* Silvana, Milan 1953: catalogue of the Milan exhibition in which 350 items were on show, including painting, sculpture, ceramics and graphic work. G. White and Roland Penrose, *Picasso,* The Tate Gallery, London 1960: catalogue with 270 illustrations of pictures. J. Leymarie, R. Arnould, A. Cacan, *Hommage à Pablo Picasso,* Ministère de la Culture, Paris 1966-7: catalogue for Picasso's eighty-fifth birthday exhibition, with 284 illustrations of paintings and 508 other illustrations of sculpture, ceramics and drawings.

Essays and Articles

Guillaume Apollinaire, ' Les jeunes, Picasso peintre ', *La Plume,* Paris 15 May 1905; A. Salmon, *La jeune peinture française,* Société des Trente, Paris 1919; Umberto Boccioni, ' Che cosa ci divide dal cubismo ', in *Pittura, scultura futuriste,* Edizioni futuriste di Poesia, Milan 1914; Aragon, *La peinture au défi,* Paris 1930; M. Raphael, *Proudhon, Marx, Picasso,* Paris 1933; Paul Eluard, ' Je parle de ce qui est bien ', *Donner à Voir,* Gallimard, Paris 1939; Carlo Carrà, Ernesto Prampolini, Giulio Severini, A. Soffici, *Cinquanta disegni di P. Picasso,* Posizione, Novara 1943; Xaver Gonzalez, ' Notes from Picasso's studio ', *New Masses,* New York 19 December 1944; S. Solmi, *Disegni di Picasso,* Hoepli, Milan 1945; C. Brandi, *Carmine o della pittura,*

Vallecchi, Florence 1947; C. L. Ragghianti, 'Picasso e l'astrattismo', *Firenze e il mondo*, Florence April 1948; Giulia Veronesi, 'Sculture di Picasso', *Emporium*, April 1951; L. Venturi, Catalogue of the Rome Exhibition, 1953; C. Brandi, 'L'ultimo Picasso', *Nuovi Argomenti*, Rome November 1953; G. C. Argan, 'Moralismo di Picasso', *Società*, Rome September 1953; R. Guttuso, 'L'insegnamento di Picasso', *La Biennale*, Venice April 1953; Tristan Tzara, *Picasso e la poesia,* Rome 1953; Bernard Berenson, 'Picasso', *Corriere della Sera*, Milan 24 December 1953; D.-H. Kahnweiler, *Mes galeries et mes peintres*, Paris 1961; M. De Micheli, 'Picasso', *I protagonisti*, Milan July 1965; E. Quinn and R. Penrose, *Picasso à l'oeuvre*, Paris 1965.

Goat (see note on p. 37)

Notes on the Plates

1 Divan, 1900. Coloured drawing, 25 × 29 cm. Signed at bottom right 'P. Ruiz Picasso'. Barcelona, Museo Picasso. The influence of Parisian artists, from Stenlein to Toulouse-Lautrec, is already apparent here.

2 Bibi la purée, 1901. Oil on panel, 49 × 39 cm. Signed Picasso at bottom right. Paris, private collection. This is one of the works painted in a violent and instinctive neo-impressionist technique.

3 Dwarf Dancer, 1901 (La Nana). Oil on canvas, 104 × 61 cm.; signed 'Picasso' at bottom left. Barcelona, Museo Picasso. This is one of the neo-impressionist works, like the one above.

4 Painted Woman (L'Attente), 1901. Oil, 69 × 56 cm. Signed 'Picasso' at bottom left. Barcelona, Museo Picasso. This belongs to the same group as the two preceding paintings. The subject matter is inspired by Lautrec but already, both in the attitude and in the mournful gentleness of the figure, there is a foretaste of the 'blue period'. It is one of Picasso's earliest masterpieces.

5 Sick Child, 1903. Tempera, 46 × 40 cm. Barcelona, Museo Picasso. This belongs to the middle of the 'blue period'; it was begun in Paris at the end of 1901 and completed in Barcelona the following year.

6 Embracing Lovers, 1903. Pastel, 98 × 57 cm., signed 'Picasso' at top right. Paris, Orangerie. Picasso was working on this subject by at least 1901. It is a subject which has produced one of the most beautiful of the 'blue period' paintings: *Life*.

7 The Old Jew, 1903. Oil on canvas. 125 × 92 cm.; signed at top right. Moscow, Museum of Modern Western Art. A typical work of the 'blue period'.

8 Woman With Crow, 1904. Tempera and pastel, 65 × 50 cm.; signed and dated. Toledo Museum of Art. Picasso made a replica of this painting a few days later, which remained unknown until the Paris exhibition held on the occasion of his eighty-fifth birthday.

9 Couple, 1904. Oil on canvas, 100 × 81 cm.; signed at bottom right. Ascona, Switzerland, B. Mayer Collection. Also known by the title *Les Misérables*.

10 Harlequin's Family, 1905. Tempera 58 × 44 cm., Signed and dated at bottom right. New York, Metropolitan Museum of Art. This is one of the 'pink period' paintings.

The Jester, 1905 (*ill. on p. 9*). Bronze, 40 × 35 cm.; signed and dated on the back. Paris, Musée de l'Art Moderne. Picasso's interest in sculpture began in the early 1900s, as can be seen from the *Seated Woman* of 1901, *The Blind Singer* and the *Head of a Picador with Broken Nose* of 1903. *The Jester*, modelled impressionistically, takes its place among the 'pink period' subjects.

11 Seated Saltimbanque With Boy, 1906. Tempera on cardboard, 100 × 70 cm.; signed at bottom right. Zurich, Kunsthaus. Painted towards the end of the 'pink period'.

12 Portrait of Gertrude Stein, 1906. Oil on canvas, 100 × 81 cm. New York, Metropolitan Museum of Art. Gertrude Stein posed for Picasso during the whole winter of 1906: eighty sittings. Picasso was still not satisfied, and destroyed the head. He painted it again some time later without a model. With this work, Picasso left the 'pink period' completely behind him, and was moving towards a new artistic experience.

13 The Maids of Avignon, 1907. Oil on canvas, 99 × 99 cm. New York, Museum of Modern Art. A key painting in the history of modern art. This work marks Picasso's encounter with the 'primitive'. Its title was originally *Brothel of Avignon*, and its present title was bestowed by the poet André Salmon.

14 Nude and Drapery, 1907. Oil on canvas, 152 × 101 cm.; Leningrad, Hermitage Museum.

15 Male Nude, 1908. Oil on canvas, 92 × 73 cm.; signed at top right. Private collection.

16 Three Seated Women, 1907-8. Oil on canvas, 99 × 99 cm. London, Douglas Cooper Collection.

17 Water Reservoir, 1909. Oil on canvas, 81 × 64 cm. Paris, Private collection. This work was painted at Horta de Ebro and is one of the outstanding examples of the first, 'heroic' phase of cubism.

Head of Woman (*ill. on p. 17*). Bronze, height 41 cm. New York, Museum of Modern Art. The sculpture belongs to the early stages of cubism, and shows the transition from 'Negro' schematic forms to the more angular and complex forms of the new style.

18 Mandoline Player, 1911. Oil on canvas, 97 × 70 cm. Liège, Graindorge Collection. Like the two following works, this belongs to the period of 'analytical cubism'.

19 Spanish Still-Life, 1912. Oil on canvas, 46 × 33, cm.; signed on the back. Private collection.

20 Woman with Guitar, 1912 (Ma Jolie). Oil on canvas, 95 × 70 cm. New York, Museum of Modern Art. The title is taken from a line of a popular song of the time: '*O Manon, ma jolie, mon coeur te dit bonjour*'.

21 Violin, 1913. Oil on canvas, 81 × 54 cm.; signed and dated on the back, with the inscription: '*Sur une table, un violon, un verre et une bouteille*' ('On a table, a violin, a glass and a bottle'). Lucerne, Siegfried Rosengart Collection. This painting, like the two following, belongs to the period of 'synthetic cubism'.

22 Woman in an Armchair, 1913. Oil on canvas, 150 × 100 cm.; signed and dated on the reverse. Florence, Signora Ingeborg Pudelko Collection. This is one of the most famous paintings of this period.

23 Guitar, Skull and Newspaper, 1914. Oil on canvas, 40 × 70 cm. London, R. Penrose Collection.

24 Italian Woman, 1917. Oil on canvas, 149 × 101 cm.; signed and dated, with the name of the place where it was painted (Rome) at the top left. Zurich, E. G. Bührle Foundation. This painting was produced at the beginning of what has been called Picasso's 'great cubist period'.

25 Harlequin with Guitar, 1918. Tempera on wood, 35 × 27 cm.; signed and dated at bottom right. Paris, Berggruen Collection. This belongs to the 'neoclassical period', which began the previous year.

26 Chest of Drawers, 1919. Oil on canvas, 81 × 100 cm. Property of the artist.

27 Glass, Flowers, Guitar and Bottle, 1919. Oil on canvas, 100 × 81 cm.; signed and dated at bottom left. Paris, Berggruen Collection.

28 Composition, 1919. Oil on canvas, 60 × 80 cm. Private collection.

29 Three Musicians, 1921. Oil on canvas, 204 × 223 cm. New York, Museum of Modern Art. This work marks the culmination of the period of 'great cubism'. A work of equal dimensions and on the same subject is in Philadelphia Museum of Modern Art.

30 Mother and Child, 1922. Oil on canvas, 97 × 61 cm. New York, Alex L. Hillmann Collection.

31 Still-life with Guitar, 1922. Oil on canvas, 83 × 102 cm.; signed and dated at bottom left. Lucerne, Siegfried Rosengart Collection. During the period of 'great cubism' which developed simultaneously with the 'neoclassical period', Picasso produced large numbers of still-lifes, conceived in broad planes and on a very large scale.

32 Seated Harlequin, 1923. Oil on canvas, 130 × 97 cm. Berne, Kunstmuseum.

33 Birdcage, 1923. Oil on canvas, 200 × 140 cm.; signed at bottom left. New York, Victor W. Ganz Collection.

34 Musical Instruments, 1923. Oil on canvas, 85 × 110 cm. Patrick C. Hill Collection.

35 Still-life with Guitar, 1924. Oil on canvas, 97½ × 130 cm; signed and dated. Amsterdam, Stedelijk Museum.

36 Paul as Pierrot, 1925. Oil on canvas, 130 × 97 cm.; dated on the frame. This is a portrait of the artist's son at the age of four. There are two other portraits of his son Paul aged four: *Paul as a Bullfighter* and *Paul as Pierrot with a Bouquet.* The last-named was painted four years after the two others. There are also three portraits of Paul at the age of two, and one at three: *Paul as Harlequin.*

37 Seated Woman, 1941. Oil on canvas, 92 × 73 cm. Property of the author.

38 The Red Armchair, 1931. Oil and enamel on plywood, 130× 97 cm. Property of the artist.

Head (*ill. on p. 22*). Bronze, 84 × 40 × 36 cm. Property of the artist.

Cock, 1932 (*ill. on p. 27*). Bronze, 66 × 61 × 33 cm. Property of the artist.

39 Bathers, 1937. Oil on canvas, 130 × 195 cm.; dated on the reverse. Venice, Guggenheim Collection. This is an example of a series of paintings described by some critics as the ' crystal period '. These works began to appear after 1925, after Picasso came into contact with the surrealists. Medusa-like figures, like polished piles of wasted bones, obviously referring to the erotic unconscious. The primordial joy of certain of Picasso's neoclassical images of femininity was followed by these disturbing and sometimes cruel pictures.

40 Portrait of Dora Maar, 1937. Oil on canvas, 92 × 65 · cm.; dated on the frame. Property of the artist.

41 Head of a Horse, 1937. Oil on canvas, 65 × 92 cm. New York, Museum of Modern Art. Dated at the top left: 2 May 1937. This painting was therefore produced four days after the bombardment of Guernica, and is a study for the painting of that subject.

42-3 Guernica, 1937. Tempera on canvas, 351.0 × 782.5 cm. On loan to the Museum of Modern Art, New York.

44 Weeping Woman, 1937. Oil on canvas, 60 × 49 cm. Signed and dated on right; also dated on the frame: 26 October, 1937. London, Antony Penrose Collection. This is part of the *Guernica* series.

45 Still-life with Black Bull, Book, Palette and Candlestick, 1938. Oil on canvas, 97 × 130 cm.; signed and dated at top right. Saint-Jean-de-Gonville, Colonel Valdemar Ebbesen Collection.

46 Portrait of Maia with Doll, 1938. Oil on canvas, 37 × 69 cm.; dated at bottom left 16 January 1938. Property of the author. In this portrait Picasso's daughter Maia is two-and-a-half years old. There exists another portrait of Maia at the same age, holding a toy boat.

47 Still-life with Flowers, Pitcher, and Ox-skull, 1939. Oil on canvas, 80 × 100 cm. Munich, Staatsgalerie.

48 Portrait of Madame Eluard, 1941. Oil on canvas, 72×60 cm.; Paris, Museum of Modern Art.

49 Seated Woman, 1941. Oil on canvas, 92 × 73 cm. Brussels, private collection. This is one of the many paintings of *Seated Women* produced during the war years.

50-1 The Three Ages of Man, 1942. Oil on panel, 54 × 65 cm.; signed and dated at bottom left November 1942. Brussels, Marcel Mabille Collection. This painting shows how Picasso kept returning to mythical and neoclassical subjects.

52 Still-life with Ox-skull, 1942. Oil on canvas, 130 × 97 cm.; signed at bottom right and dated 6 April 1942.

53 Seated Woman with Fish Hat, 1942. Oil on canvas, 100 × 81 cm. Amsterdam, Stedelijk Museum.

54 Seated Woman, 1942. Oil on canvas, 100 × 80 cm. Property of the artist.

55 Bust of Woman in a Blue Hat, 1944. Oil on canvas, 92 × 60 cm. Property of the artist.

Man with Lamb, 1944 (*ill. on p. 29*). Bronze, 220 × 78 × 72 cm. Vallauris, Place de l'Hôtel de Ville. For this work, which is one of his greatest sculptures, Picasso executed large numbers of preliminary sketches between July 1942 and October 1943. It is an image of peace conceived in the darkest days of the war.

Skull, 1944 (*ill. on p. 29*). Bronze, 29 × 22 × 26 cm. Property of the artist.

56   The Enamel Saucepan, 1945. Oil on canvas, 82 × 165 cm.; dated on the frame. Paris, Museum of Modern Art.

57   Head of Girl, 1949. Oil on canvas, 61 × 50 cm. Turin, private collection.

Goat, 1950 (*ill. on p. 31*). Bronze, 121 × 73 × 149 cm. Property of the artist. This sculpture is composed of various ' *objets trouvés* ', which define its structure: a palm branch models the spine; a basket, the ribs; two gourds, the udders; fragments of iron and wood, the other parts of the body. This is an elemental metamorphic conception which dominates many of Picasso's sculptures, a kind of rudimentary dialectic of nature, in which an object becomes other than itself, a ' dead object ' is brought to life again and incorporated into a new aspect of existence. The most obvious example of such a ' metamorphosis ' is to be found in Picasso's *Head of a Bull*, 1943, composed of the handlebars and saddle of a bicycle. Referring to this sculpture, Picasso said: ' I have made from this saddle and this handlebar the bull's head which everyone can recognise for what it is, a bull's head. The metamorphosis has been accomplished, and I now want another metamorphosis to take place in reverse. Suppose my head of a bull is thrown on to the scrap heap. Perhaps one day a boy will say: " Here is something which could be used as a handlebar for my bicycle. " In this way a double metamorphosis will be accomplished. '

58-9   Smoke Clouds at Vallauris, 1951. Oil on canvas, 60 × 73 cm. Property of the artist. Landscape has occupied a relatively small place in Picasso's work in comparison with his vast production of figure paintings. And it must be said that in his landscapes Picasso seems to be more cautious, as if he is holding back the energy which disintegrates and recomposes forms. Landscape painting represents for Picasso a return to a condition of natural equilibrium. He once said: ' We must go back to painting landscape with the eyes. To see a thing, it is necessary to see all things. Landscape must be painted with the eyes, and not with the prejudices which are in our heads. No matter if our eyes are closed, so long as it is with the eyes '.

60   Peace, 1952. Oil on brickwork, detail from left of composition. This work, the same size as its companion *War* (*pls 61-3*), is conceived as a return of the ' Golden Age '. The old Picasso of myth and idyll is manifest here. In this detail we see Pegasus, the symbol of poetry, pulling the plough which is guided by a child, to signify that in the Kingdom of Peace, even work will no longer be toil, but a liberation of the energies of the spirit; while above the sun shines like a diamond, like the vari-coloured eyes of a peacock's tail. Images are used in a similar way throughout this vast composition: the owl, a symbol of wisdom, standing on the head of a child; two women performing a dance in a nature freed from every menace, and a family resting happily together under a fruit-laden tree, symbol of abundance.

61-3 War, 1952. Oil on brickwork. 470 × 1020 cm. Property of the artist. This work, together with *Peace*, is in an old chapel at Vallauris, which was used during the French Revolution as an oil-press. This deconsecrated chapel was bought by Picasso, who has made it into a ' Temple of Peace '.

64 Two Children, 1952. Oil on canvas, 92 × 73 cm. Dated on the reverse 13 May 1952. Property of the artist.

Baboon with Young, 1952 (*ill. on p. 39*). Bronze, height 56 cm. Property of the artist. This is another admirable example of a ' metamorphosis ': two toy cars have been transformed into the head of an animal.

65 Woman Dressing her Hair, 1954 (La Coiffure). Oil on canvas, 55 × 30 cm. Lucerne, Siegfried Rosengart Collection.

66 Seated Woman in Turkish Costume, 1955. Oil on canvas, 100 × 80 cm. This is one of the works first exhibited in the Galerie Louise Leiris, Paris, in March-April 1957.

67 Nude before a Garden, 1956. Oil on canvas, 130 × 162 cm.; signed at top right. First exhibited together with the preceding work. Pittsburgh, Thompson Collection.

68 Woman in a Studio, 1956. Oil on canvas, 114 × 146 cm.; signed at top right. This is one of a group of works on the same subject first exhibited together with the two preceding works.

69 Seated Woman with Green Scarf, 1960. Oil on canvas, 195 × 130 cm.; signed at bottom left and dated on the back 28 March 1960. Bremen, Hertz Collection.

70-1 Luncheon on the Grass, 1960. Oil on canvas, 130 × 195 cm.; dated on the reverse 3 March 1960, 20 August 1960. Property of the artist. This is one of the works painted after Manet's famous work. In 1954-5, Picasso produced fourteen variations on Delacroix' *Women of Algiers*, and in 1958-9 as many as forty-five works based on Velazquez' *Las Meninas*.

72 Luncheon on the Grass, 1961. Oil on canvas, 80 × 60 cm.; signed at bottom left. Lucerne, Rosengart Collection. More than twenty-five variations on this theme, as well as many drawings, were produced by Picasso between August 1959 and September 1961.

73 Rape of the Sabines, 1962. Oil on canvas, 96 × 130 cm. Referring to the paintings and studies he produced in relation to this subject, on which he worked at Mougins in 1962-3, Picasso said: ' This is certainly not Delacroix. It lies between Poussin and David. There is not the slightest connection. Perhaps they are the Innocents, perhaps the Sabine Women '. The allusion is to Poussin's

Massacre of the Innocents and David's *Rape of the Sabines*. With this painting, inspired this time by the art of the past rather than by present-day violence, Picasso returned to the theme of *Guernica* and the *Massacre in Korea* which he had painted in 1951: he returned, in fact, to one of the fundamental aspects of his creative dialectic. This was certainly not a matter of chance, just as it was not by chance that he had turned to the *Women of Algiers*. The time of massacres, alas, is not past.

74-5 Still-life with Cat and Lobster, 1962. Oil on canvas, 130×162 cm.; dated at bottom right 23 October 1962. Trieste, Guglielmi Collection.

76 Woman with Dog under a Tree, 1962. Oil on canvas, 160 × 130 cm. Paris, Galerie Louise Leiris. Picasso has painted a number of variations on this theme as well. It is a portrait of his wife Jacqueline with her dog Kaboul.

77 Artist and Model, 1963. Oil on canvas, 130 × 162 cm.

78-9 Artist and Model, 1963. Oil on canvas, 65 × 80 cm.; signed at top right. This is a subject which has always particularly interested Picasso. He began work on this subject in February 1963 and continued for the next few months, producing over forty paintings.

*Baboon with Young
(see note on p. 38)*

1

6

7 -

Picasso
1904

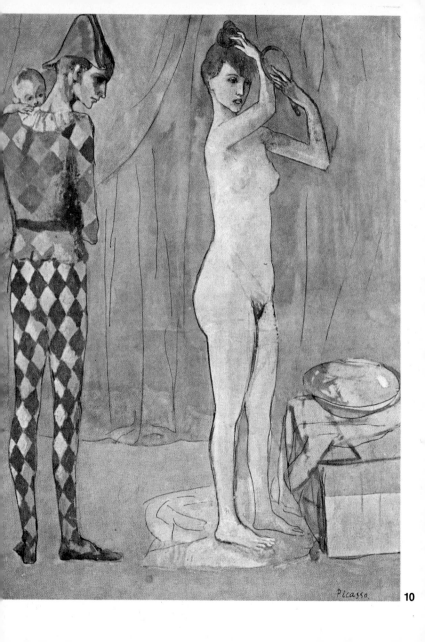

Picasso

10

18

22

23

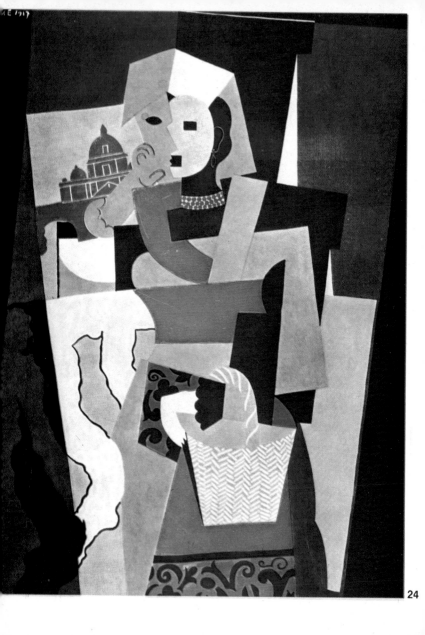

24

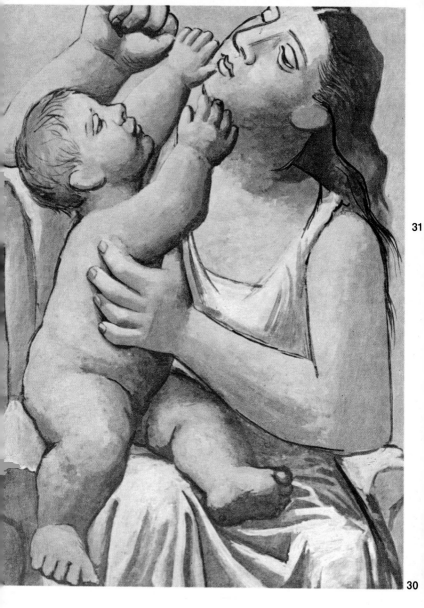

49

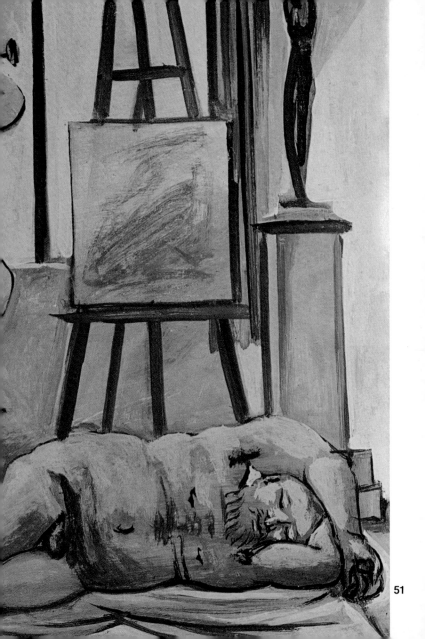

6.4.42

54

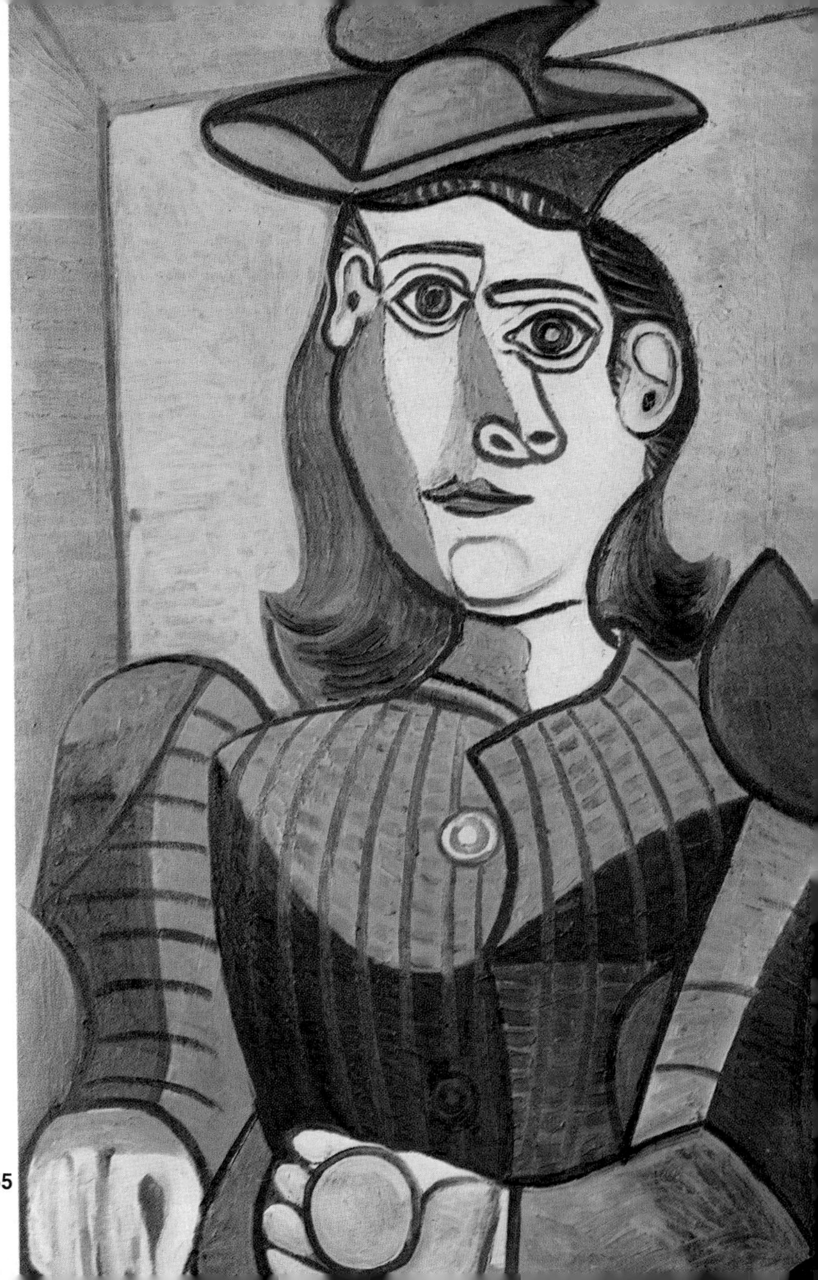

55

56

57

67

66

68

69

71

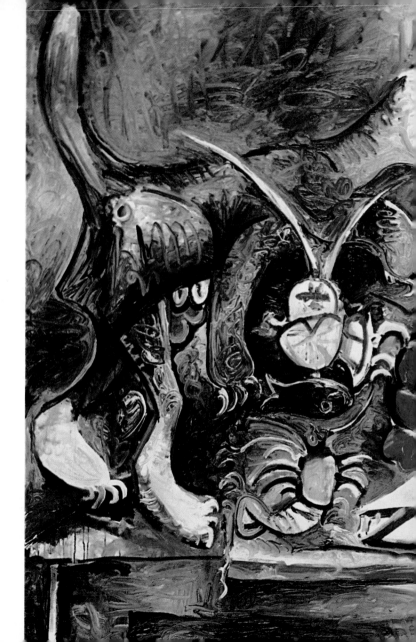

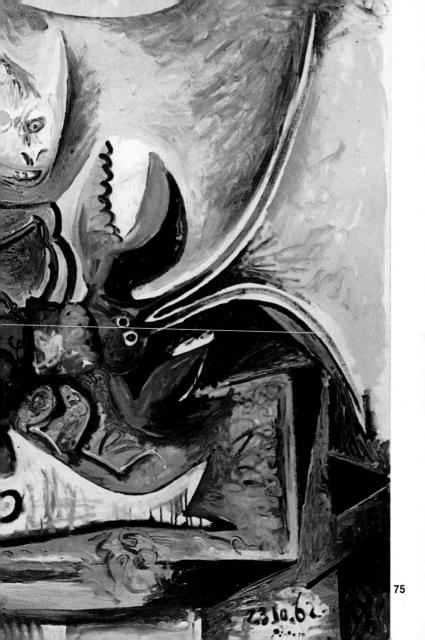

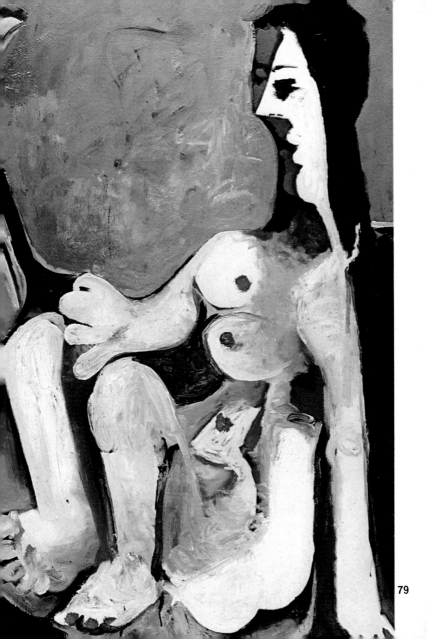

79